ENGLISH HINDI
VISUAL DICTIONARY

Tuomas Kilpi

OPPIAN

Publisher: Oppian Press
Helsinki, Finland

ISBN 978-951-877-146-6

Table of Contents • विषय-सूची

fork
कांटा
knife
चाकू
plate
थाली
spoon
चम्मच
pot
हांडी
glass
गिलास

frying pan
कड़ाही

mug
प्याला

teapot
चायदानी

strainer
छलनी

spatula
लेपनी

beans
फलियां

rice
चावल

date
खजूर

potato
आलू

tea
चाय

coffee
कॉफ़ी

apple
सेब

pear
नाशपाती

banana
केला

carrot
गाजर

sweet potato
शकरकंद

garlic
लहसुन

onion
प्याज़

pineapple
अनानास

strawberry
स्ट्रॉबेरी

orange
संतरा

coconut
नारियल

lemon
नींबू

kiwi fruit
कीवी फल

cucumber
खीरा

tomato
टमाटर

raspberry
रसभरी

grapes
अंगूर

apricot
ख़ुबानी

papaya
पपीता

melon
खरबूज़ा

plum
आलूबुखारा

mango
आम

watermelon
तरबूज़

aubergine
बैंगन

fig
अंजीर

chili
मिर्च

cauliflower
फूल गोभी

turnip
शलजम

leek
हरी प्याज़

cabbage
पत्ता गोभी

mushroom
मशरूम

lettuce
सलाद पत्ता

salt
नमक

flour
आटा

sugar
चीनी

cooking oil
खाना पकाने का तेल

margarine
नकली मक्खन

milk
दूध

cheese
पनीर

bread
डबल रोटी

pasta
पास्ता

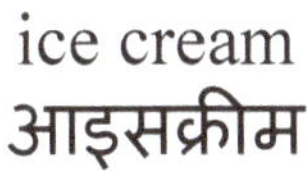

ice cream
आइसक्रीम

cookie
बिस्कुट

chocolate
चॉकलेट

hamburger
हैमबर्गर

sandwich
सैंडविच

candy
टॉफ़ी

pizza
पिज़्ज़ा

man
आदमी

woman
औरत

girl
लड़की

boy
लड़का

coat
कोट

pants
पैंट

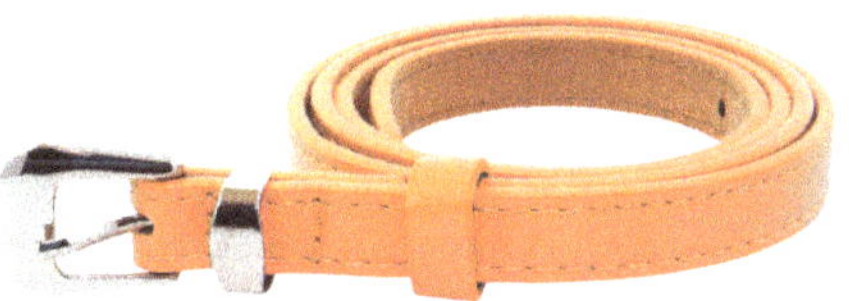

belt
बेल्ट

socks
मोज़े

shoes
जूते

shirt
शर्

skirt
स्कर्ट

scarf
स्काफ़

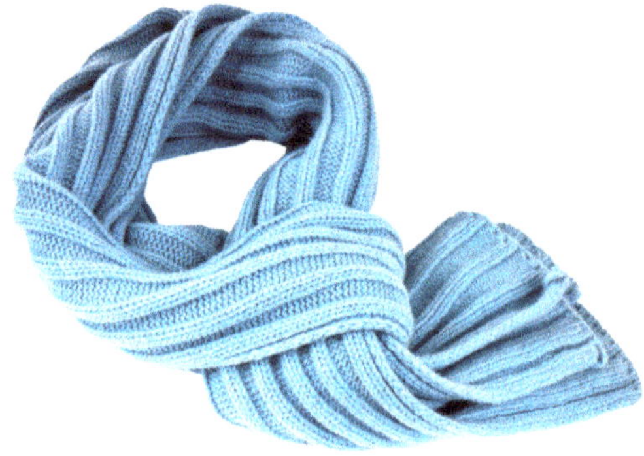

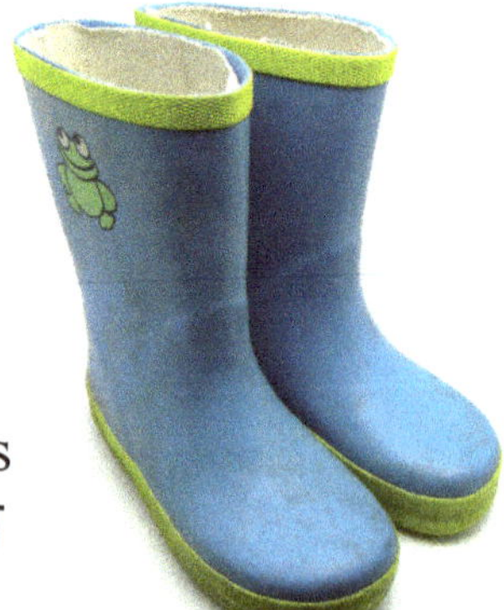

boots
बूट्स

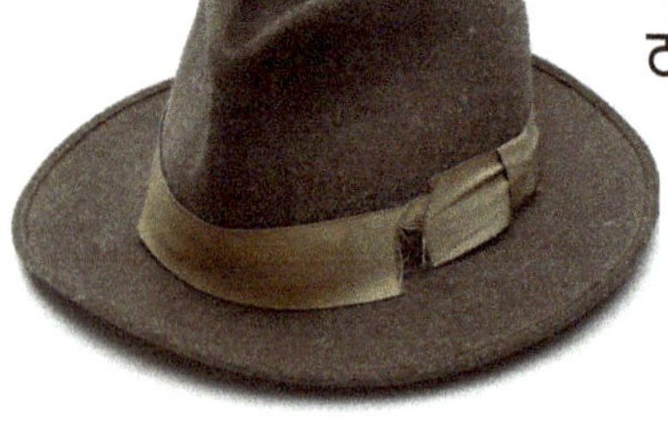

hat
टोपी

lamb
मेमना
fish
मछली
cow
गाय
cat
बिल्ली

pig
सूअर

dog
कुत्ता

chicken
मुर्गी

egg
अंडा

hare
खरगोश

bear
भालू

squirrel
गिलहरी

rat
चूहा

wolf
भेड़िया

fox
लोमड़ी

moose
मूस

snake
साँप

snail
घोंघा

spider
मकड़ी

frog
मेंढक

wasp
ततैया

bee
मधुमक्खी

fly
मक्खी

mosquito
मच्छर

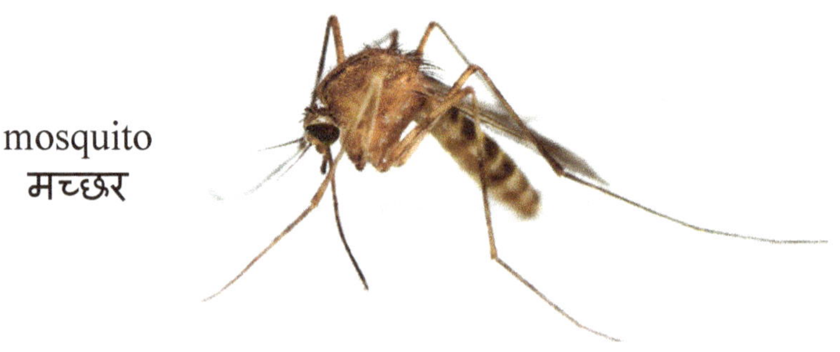

bathroom
स्नानघर

kitchen
रसोई

bedroom
शयनकक्ष

living room
बैठक कक्ष

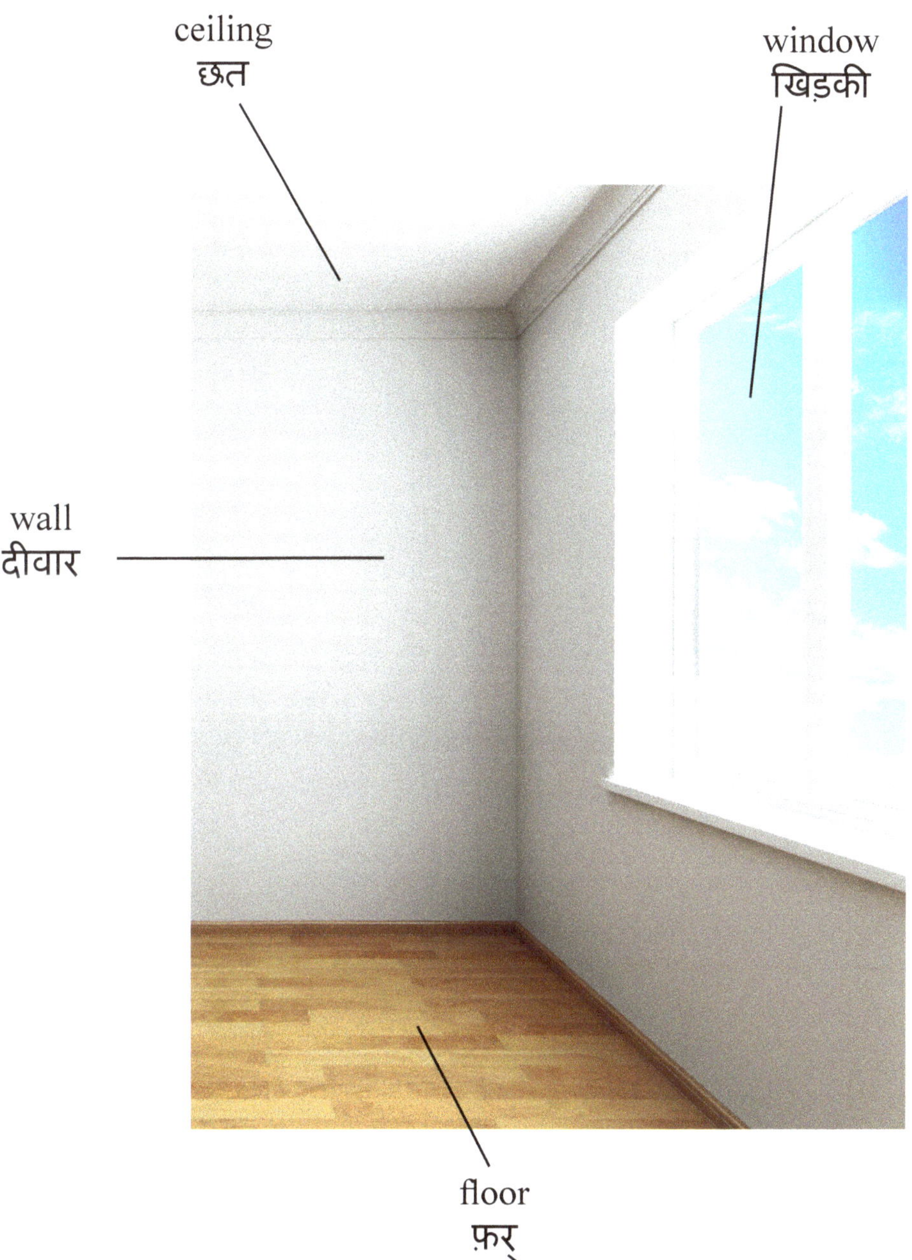
ceiling
छत
window
खिड़की
wall
दीवार
floor
फ़र्

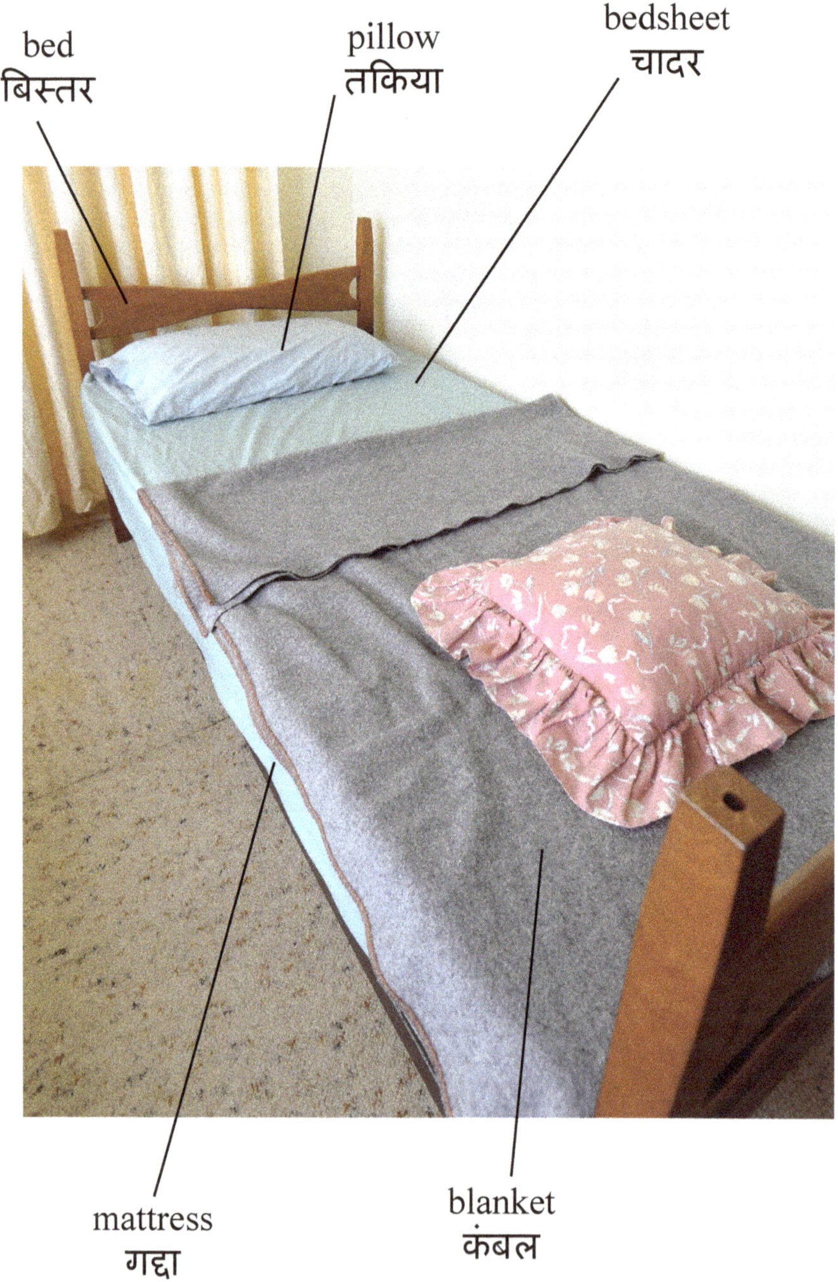

bed
बिस्तर
pillow
तकिया
bedsheet
चादर
mattress
गद्दा
blanket
कंबल

rug
गलीचा

umbrella
छतरी

lamp
लैम्प

table
मेज़

chair
कुर्सी

scissors
कैंची

envelope
लिफ़ाफ़ा

tape
टेप

parcel
पार्सल

stamp
डाक टिकट

soap
साबुन

toilet paper
टॉयलेट पेपर

toothbrush
टूथब्रश

toothpaste
टूथपेस्ट

brush
ब्रश

comb
कंघी

dental floss
डेंटल फ़्लॉस

deodorant
डिओडरेंट

scale
स्केल

electric razor
विद्युत उस्तरा

television
टेलीविज़न

remote control
रिमोट कंट्रोल

mouse
माउस

computer
कम्प्यूटर

memory stick
मेमोरी स्टिक

printer
प्रिंटर

charger
चार्जर

phone
फ़ोन

stove
स्टोव

satellite dish
सैटेलाइट डिश

headphones
हेडफ़ोन

radio
रेडियो

book
पुस्तक

flashlight
टॉर्च

shovel
खुरपा

rake
रेक

tape measure
नापने का फ़ीता

pliers
सरौता

saw
आरी

jar
जार

bottle
बोतल

can opener
कैन ओपनर

bottle opener
बोतल ओपनर

tin can
टिन का डब्बा

thread
धागा

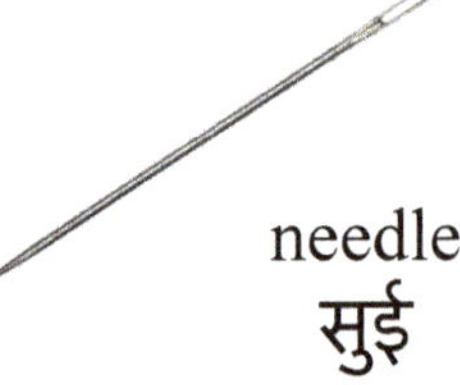

needle
सुई

refigerator
फ़्रिज

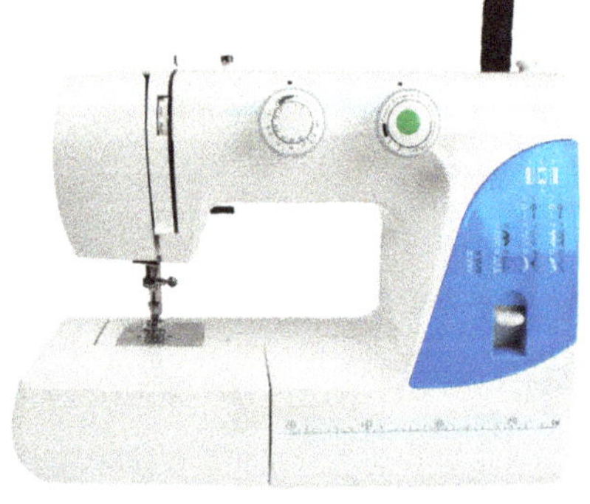

sewing machine
सिलाई मशीन

clothes peg
कपड़ों की पिन

microwave oven
माइक्रोवेव ओवन

key
चाबी

calculator
कैलकुलेटर

eyeglasses
चश्मा

electric drill
विद्युत ड्रिल
screwdriver
पेंचकस
screw
पेंच
nail
कील
hammer
हथौड़ा
wrench
पाना

credit card
क्रेडिट कार्ड

wallet
बटुआ

banknote
बैंक नोट

coin
सिक्का

passport
पासपोर्ट

timetable
समय सारणी

driving licence
ड्राइविंग लाइसेंस

fingerprint
उंगली का निशान

violin
वायलिन

saxophone
सैक्सोफ़ोन

drum
ड्रम

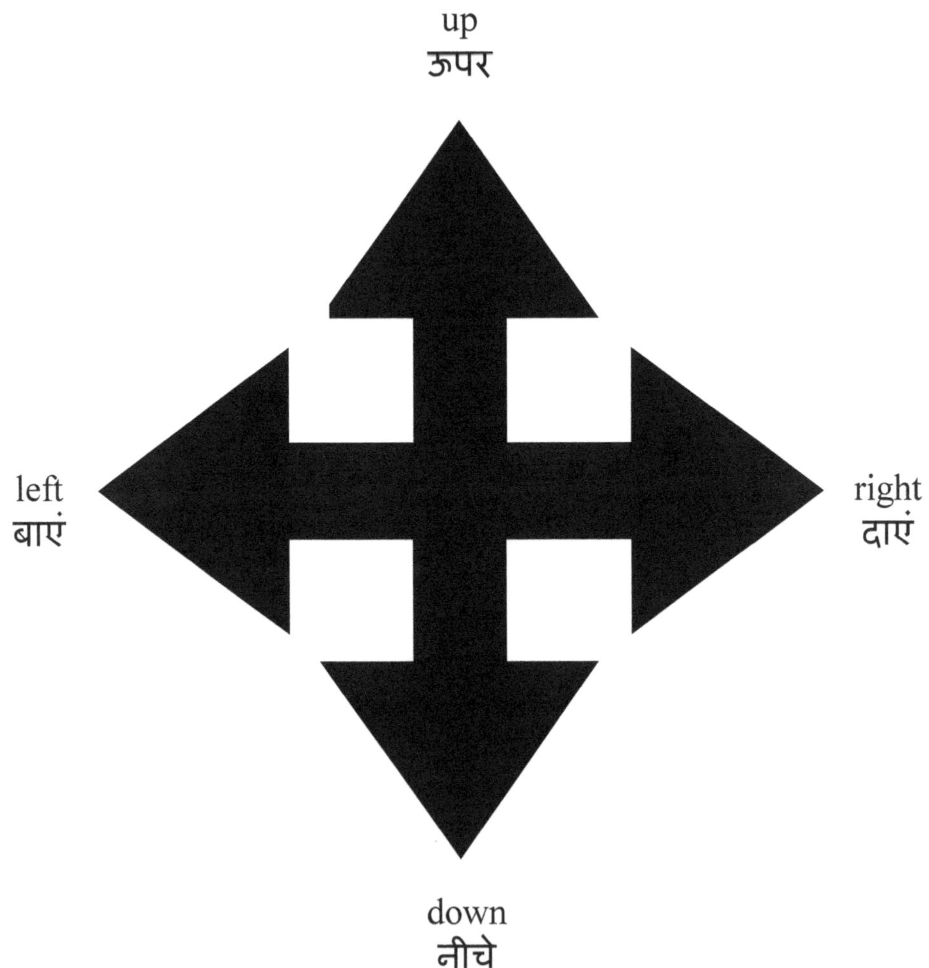
up
ऊपर
left
बाएं
right
दाएं
down
नीचे

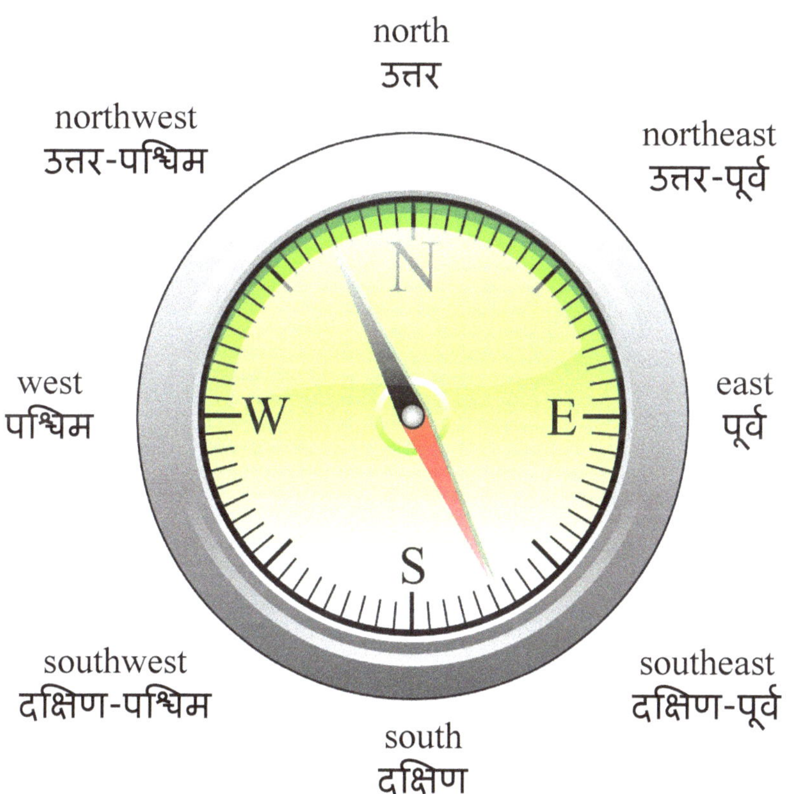

north
उत्तर
northwest
उत्तर-पश्चिम
northeast
उत्तर-पूर्व
west
पश्चिम
east
पूर्व
N
W
E
S
southwest
दक्षिण-पश्चिम
southeast
दक्षिण-पूर्व
south
दक्षिण

shoulder bag
कंधे का बैग

briefcase
ब्रीफ़केस

plastic bag
प्लास्टिक की थैली

backpack
बैकपैक

pen
कलम

pencil
पेंसिल

ruler
स्केल

notebook
नोटबुक

eraser
रबड़

car
कार

bus
बस

van
वैन

train
रेल गाड़ी

tram
ट्राम

motorcycle
मोटरसाइकिल

bicycle
साइकिल

airplane
विमान

scooter
स्कूटर

ship
समुद्री जहाज़

helicopter
हेलीकॉप्टर

truck
ट्रक

liikennevalot
traffic lights
यातायात बत्तियां

liikennemerkki
traffic sign
यातायात संकेत

suojatie
zebra crossing
ज़ेबरा क्रॉसिंग

huoltoasema
gas station
पेट्रोल पंप

bussipysäkki
bus stop
बस स्टॉप

pölynimuri
vacuum cleaner
वैक्यूम क्लीनर

moppi
mop
पोंछा

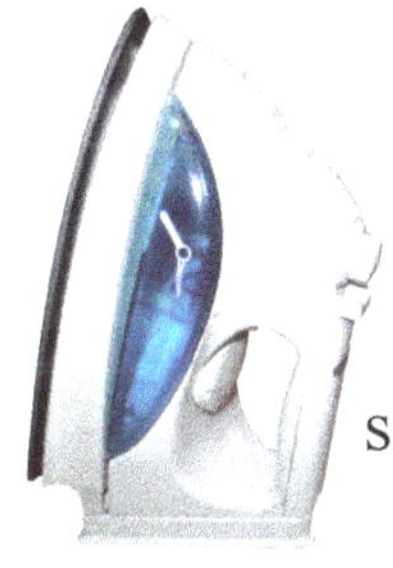

silitysrauta
smoothing iron
इस्त्री

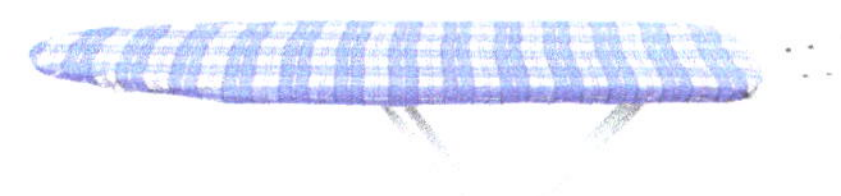

silityslauta
ironing board
इस्त्री बोर्ड

astianpesukone
dishwasher
डिश वॉशर

pesukone
washing machine
वॉशिंग मशीन

cleaning sponge
सफ़ाई स्पंज
dish brush
डिशब्रश
cleaning cloth
सफ़ाई करने का कपड़ा
dusting pan
डस्टिंग पैन
broom
झाड़ू
spray bottle
स्प्रे बोतल
bucket
बाल्टी

cot
पालना

baby rattle
झुनझुना

diaper
डायपर

pacifier
चुसनी

potty
पॉटी सीट

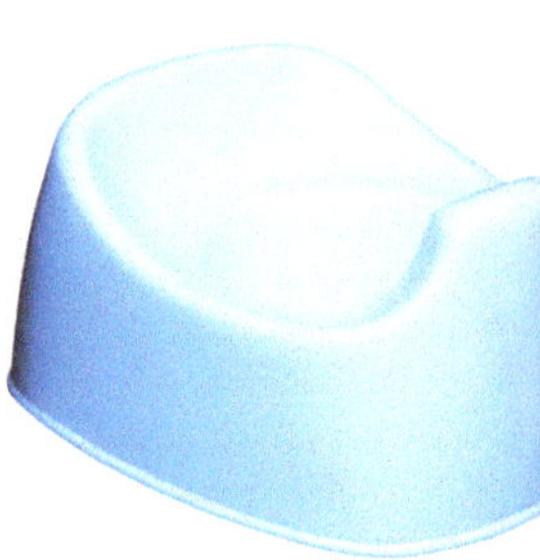

pram
प्रैम

baby bottle
बच्चे की बोतल

doll
गुड़िया

football
फ़ुटबॉल

kite
पतंग

dice
पासा

game console
गेम कंसोल

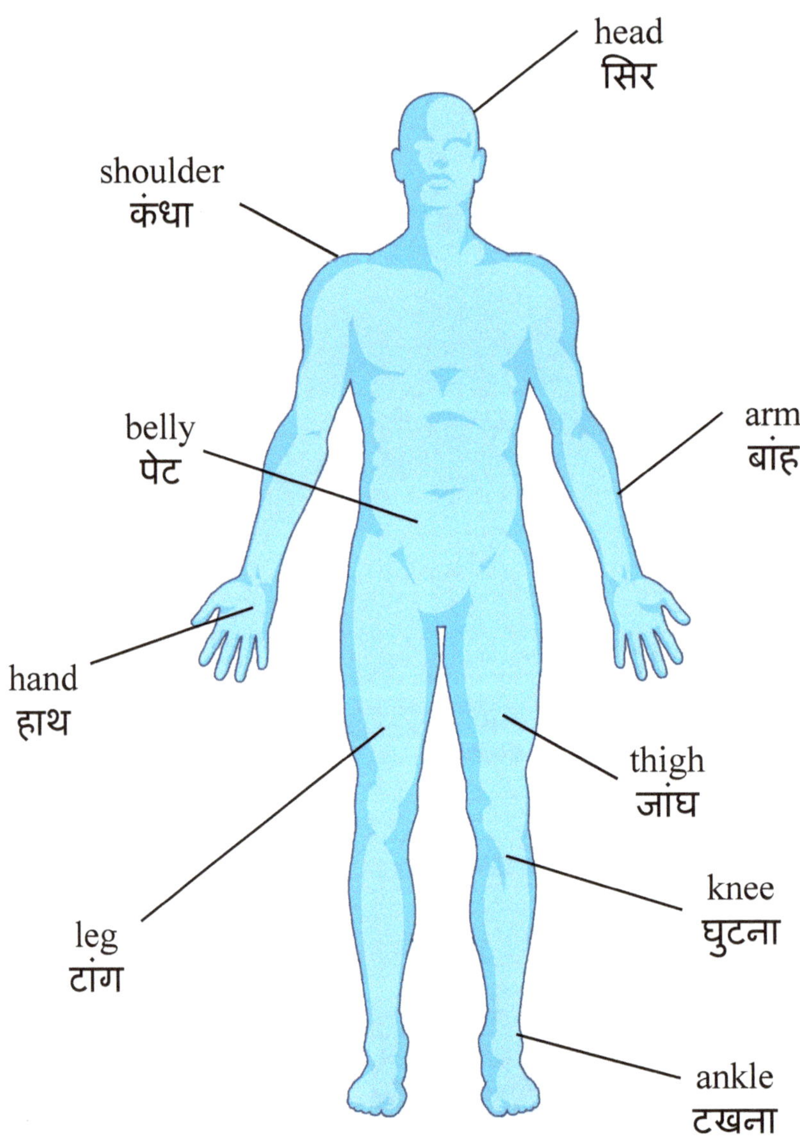

head
सिर
shoulder
कंधा
arm
बांह
belly
पेट
hand
हाथ
thigh
जांघ
leg
टांग
knee
घुटना
ankle
टखना

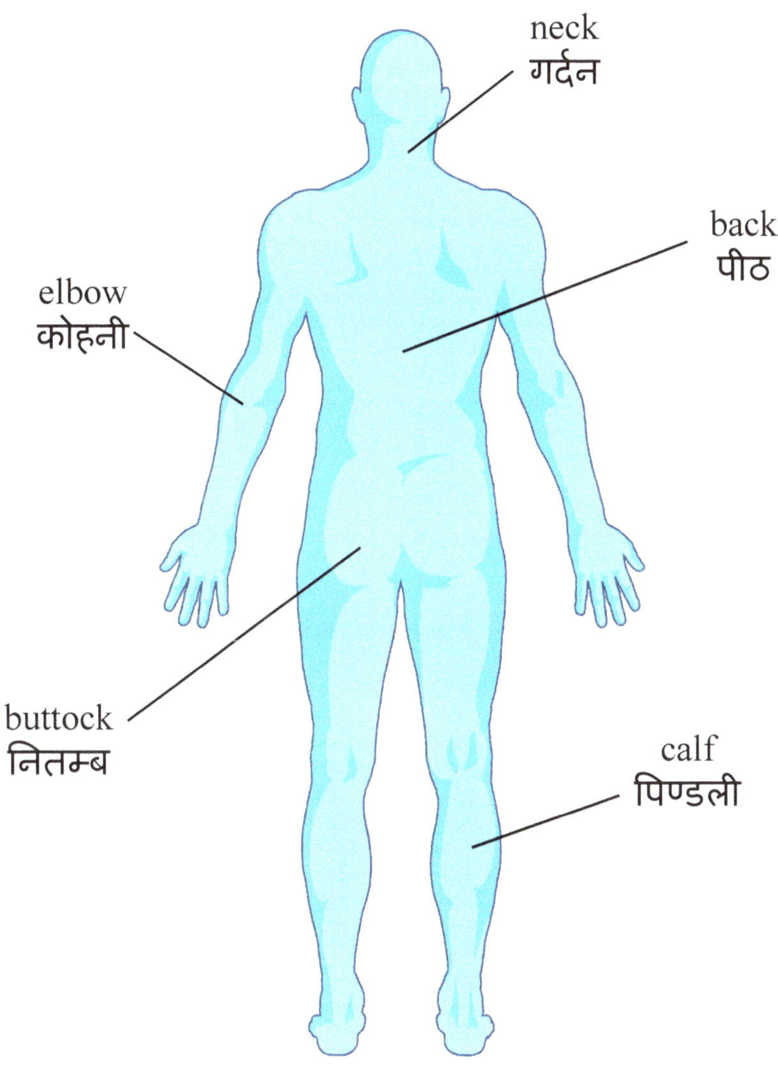

neck
गर्दन
back
पीठ
elbow
कोहनी
buttock
नितम्ब
calf
पिण्डली

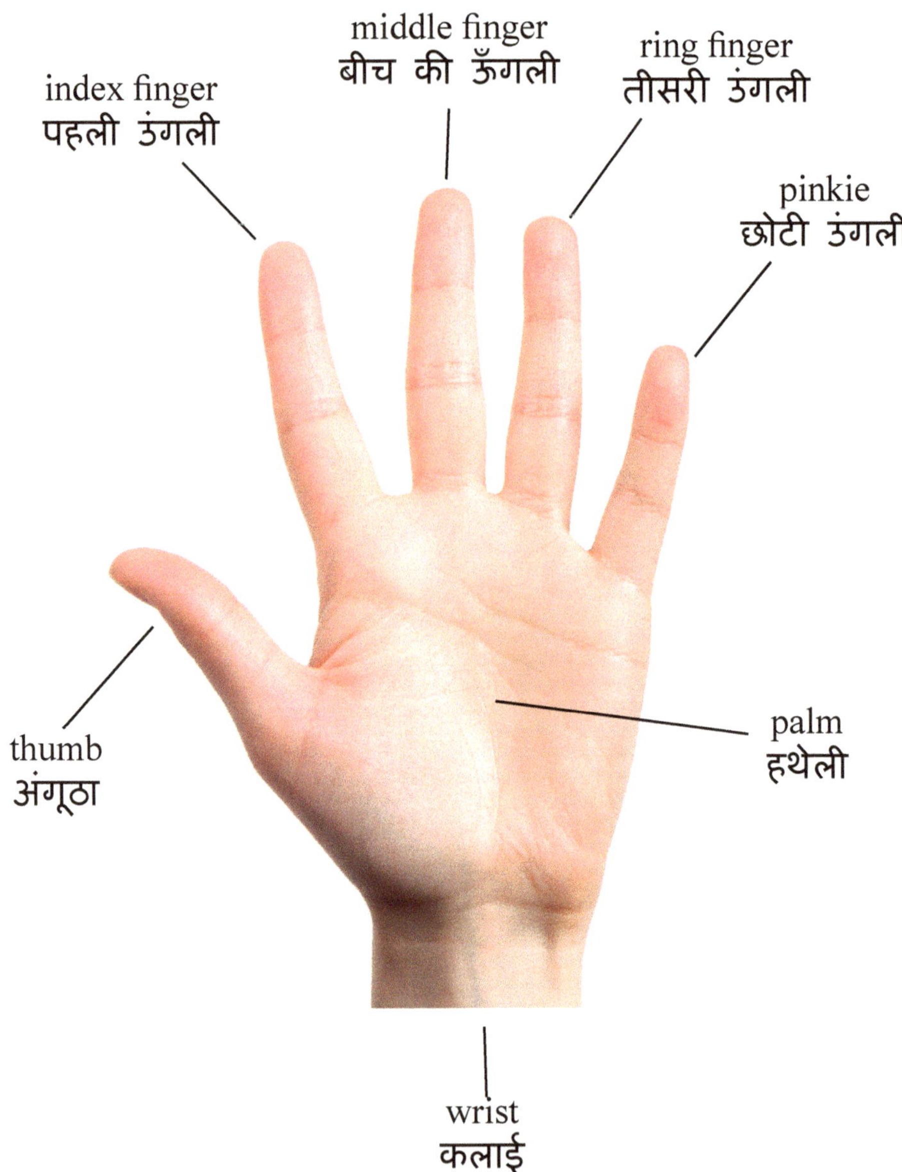
index finger
पहली उंगली
middle finger
बीच की ऊँगली
ring finger
तीसरी उंगली
pinkie
छोटी उंगली
thumb
अंगूठा
palm
हथेली
wrist
कलाई

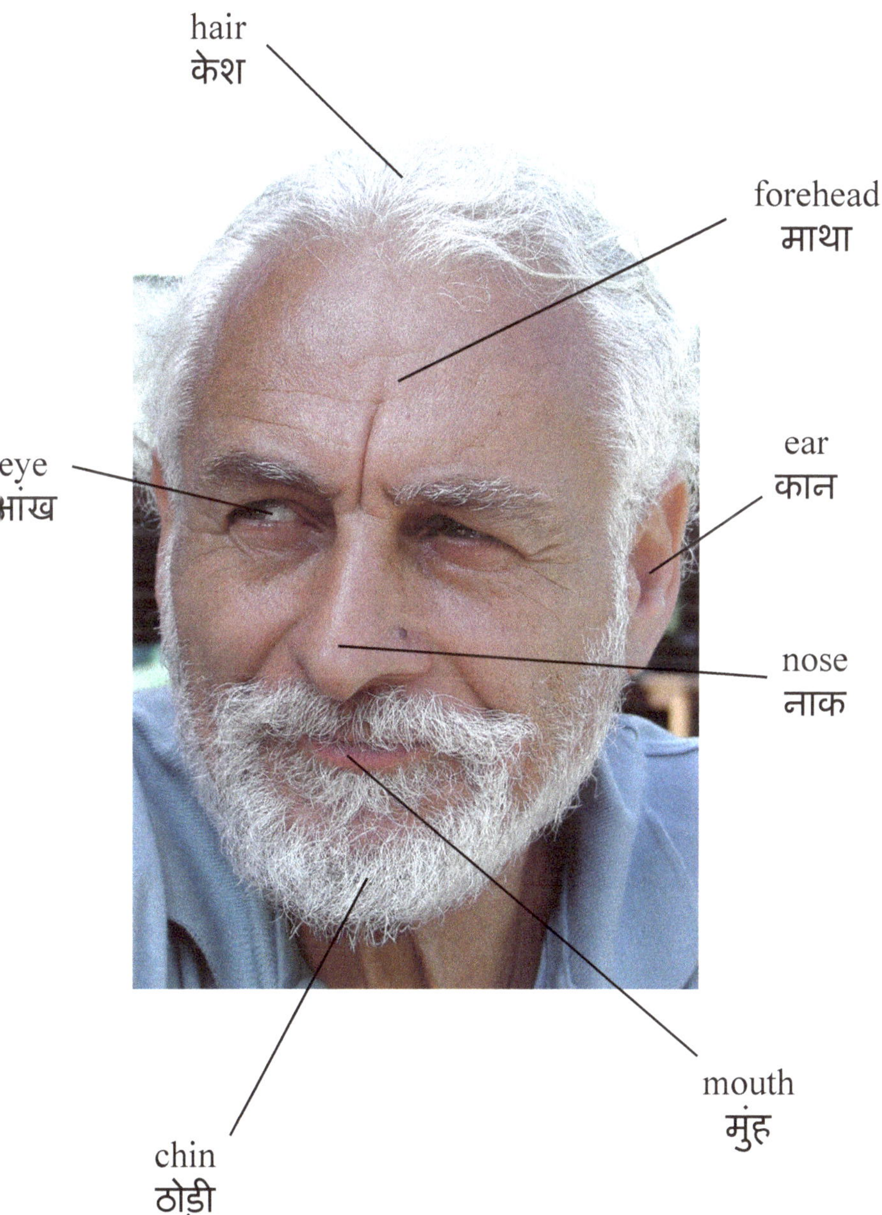

hair
केश
forehead
माथा
ear
कान
eye
आंख
nose
नाक
mouth
मुंह
chin
ठोड़ी

pharmacy
दवा की दुकान

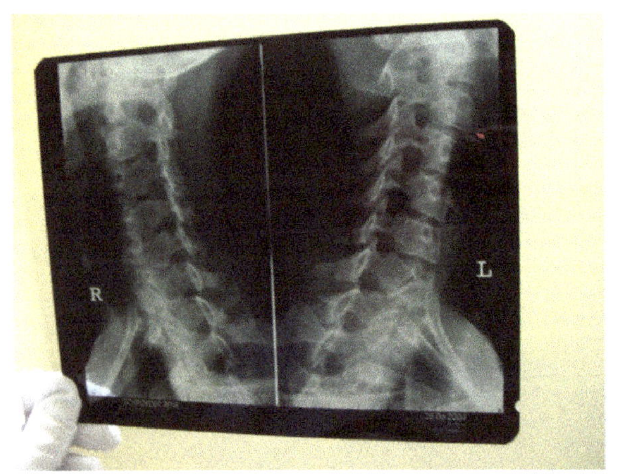

x-ray image
एक्स-रे छवि

thermometer
थर्मामीटर

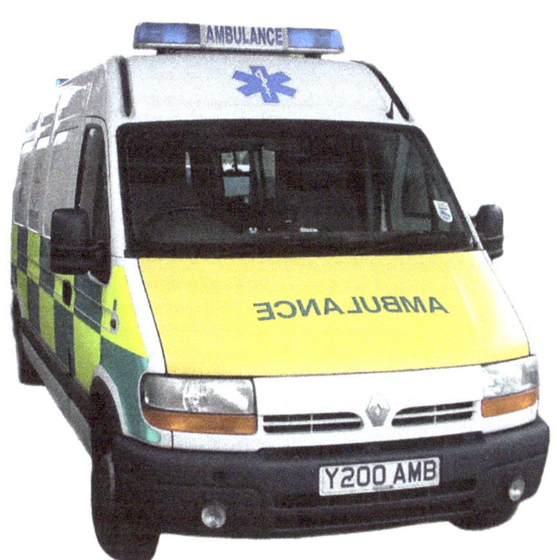

ambulance
रोगी वाहन

syringe
सुई

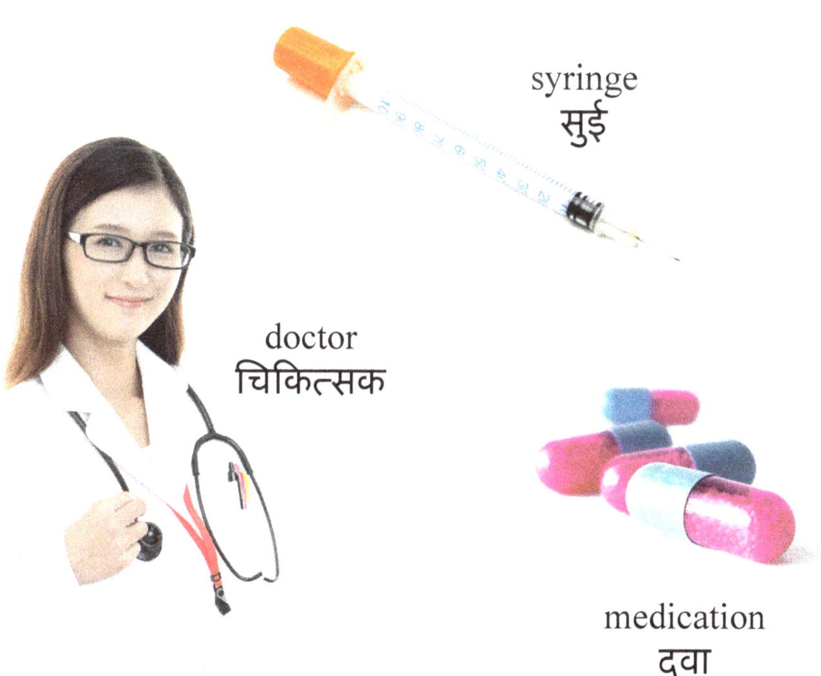

doctor
चिकित्सक

medication
दवा

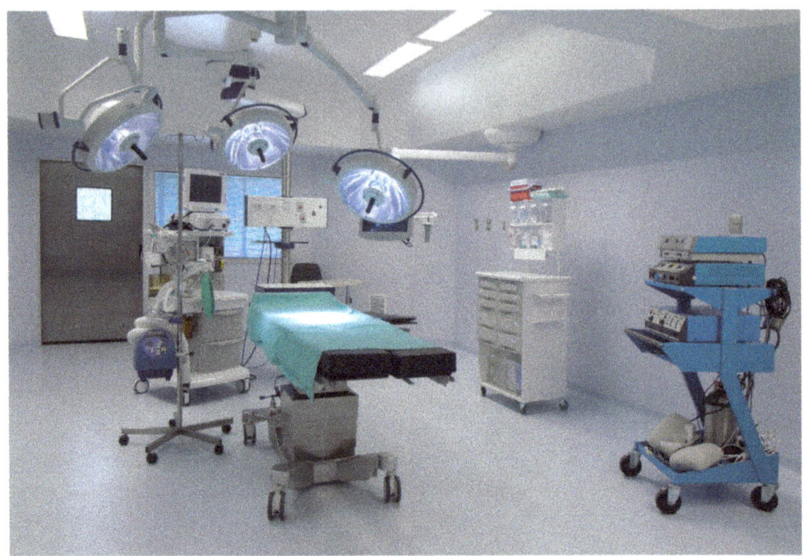

operating room
ऑपरेशन थिएटर

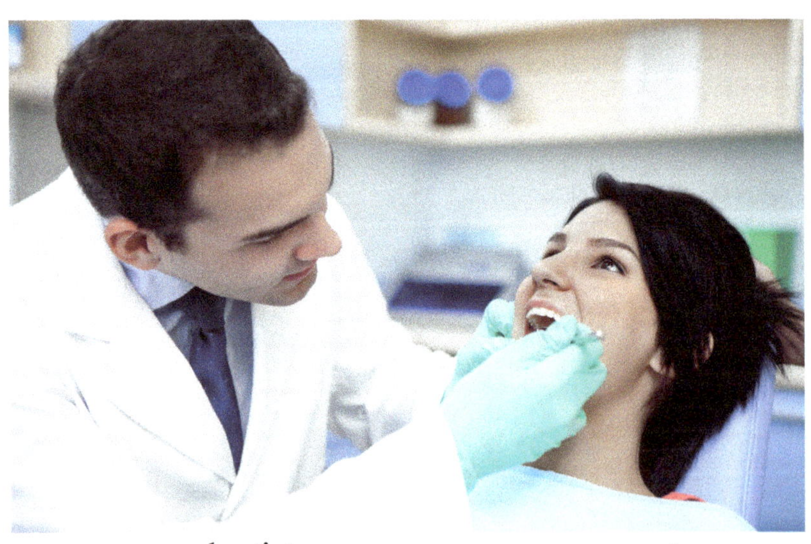

dentist
दंत चिकित्सक

patient
मरीज़

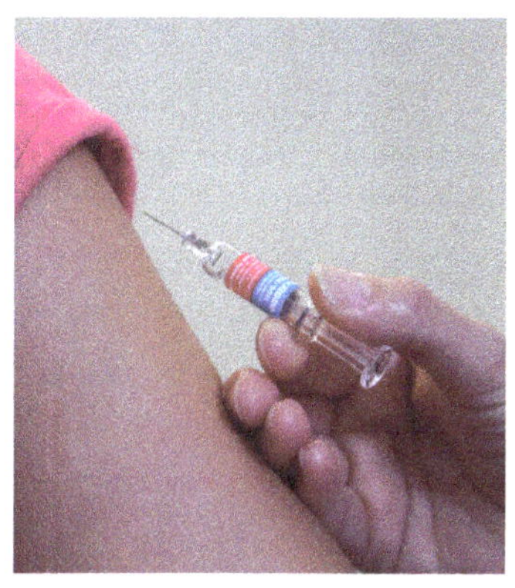

vaccination
टीका

hospital
अस्पताल

band aid
बैंड ऐड

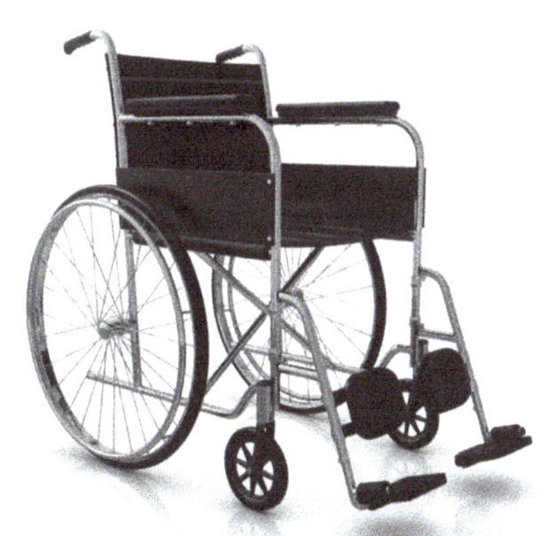

wheelchair
व्हीलचेयर

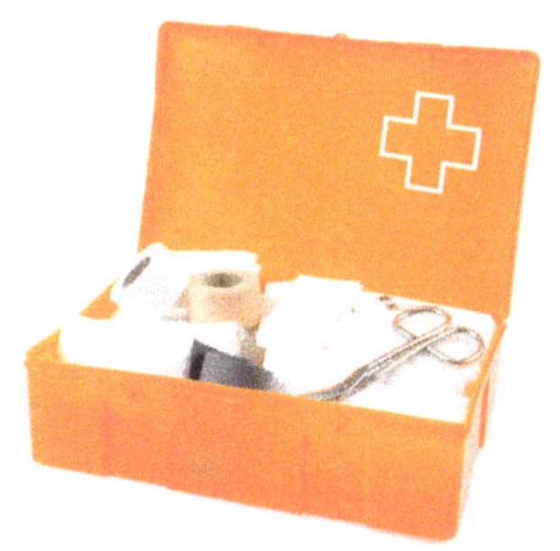

first aid kit
प्राथमिक चिकित्सा किट

to eat
खाना

to drink
पीना

to walk
पैदल चलना

to sit
बैठना

to talk
बात करना

to laugh
हंसना

to carry
उठाकर ले जाना

to stand
खड़ा होना

to smile
मुस्कुराना

to clean
साफ़ करना

to cook
पकाना

to sneeze
छींकना

to cry
रोना

to hug
गले लगाना

to sleep
सोना

to jump
कूदना

to run
भागना

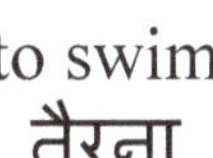

to swim
तैरना

to read
पढ़ना

to teach
सिखाना

to play
खेलना

to write
लिखना

square
चौकोर

triangle
त्रिकोण

rectangle
समकोण

circle
गोलाकार

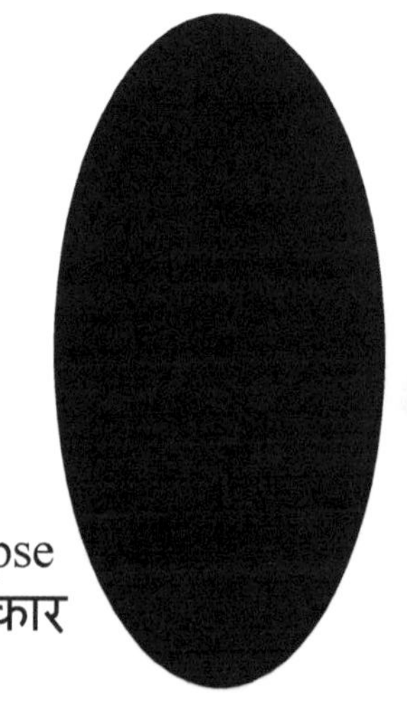

ellipse
अंडाकार

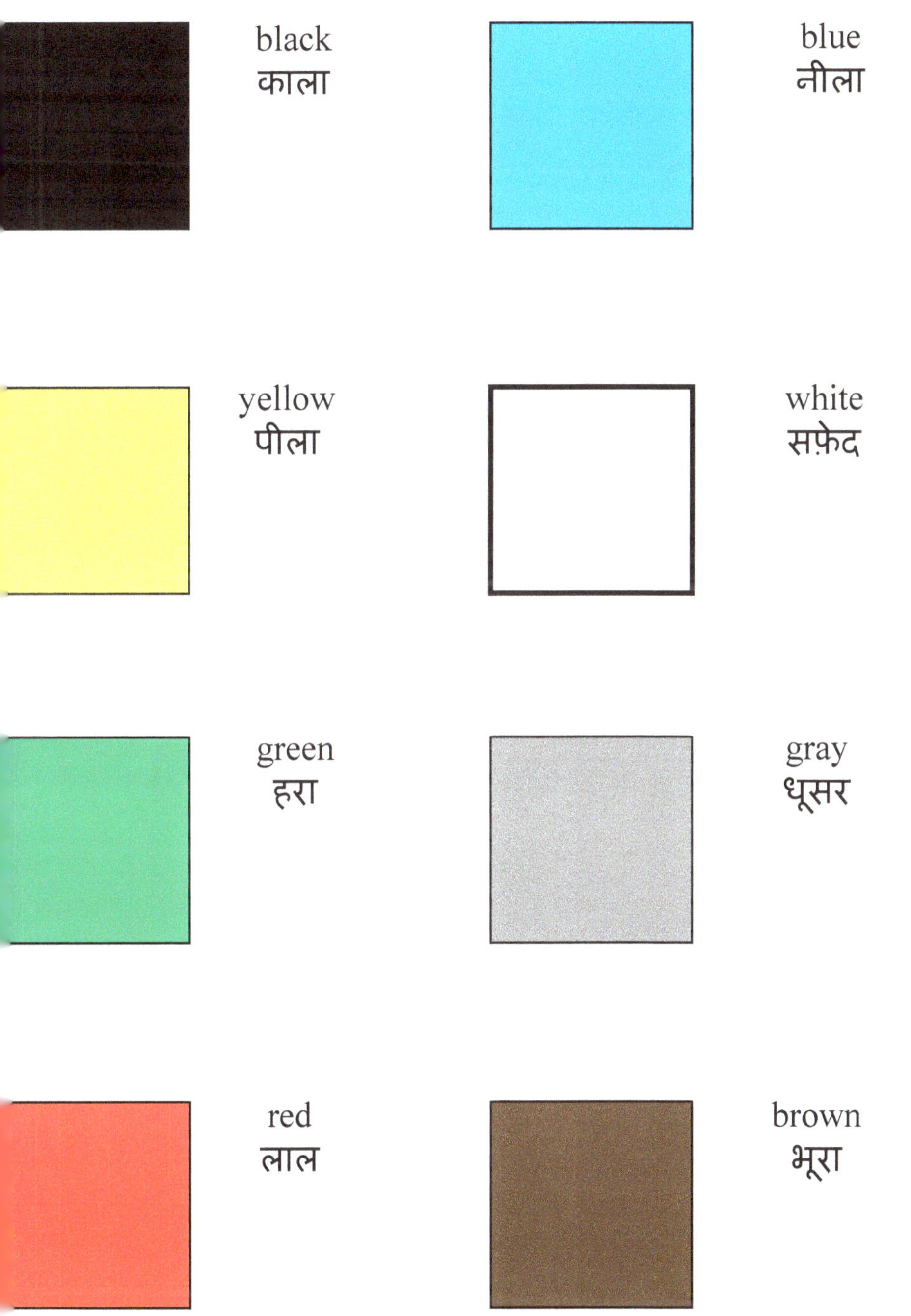

black
काला

blue
नीला

yellow
पीला

white
सफ़ेद

green
हरा

gray
धूसर

red
लाल

brown
भूरा

happy
ख़ुश

angry
गुस्सा

uncertain
अनिश्चित

surprised
आश्चर्य चकित

confused
उलझन में

supportive
मददगार

thoughtful
विचारवान

doubtful
संदेहपूर्ण

big
बड़ा

small
छोटा

fast
तेज़

slow
धीमा

good
अच्छा

bad
ख़राब

light
हल्का

heavy
भारी

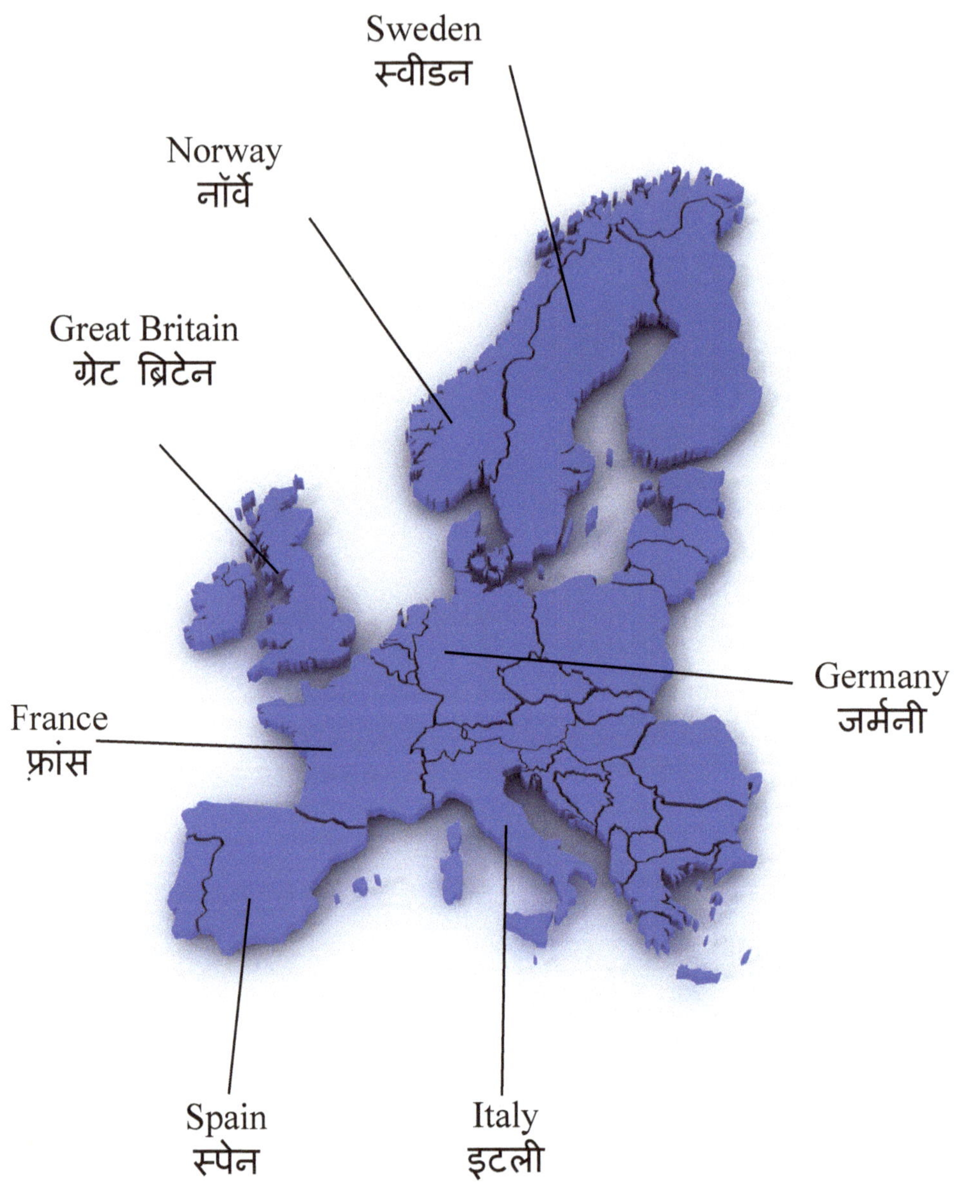

Sweden
स्वीडन
Norway
नॉर्वे
Great Britain
ग्रेट ब्रिटेन
Germany
जर्मनी
France
फ़्रांस
Spain
स्पेन
Italy
इटली

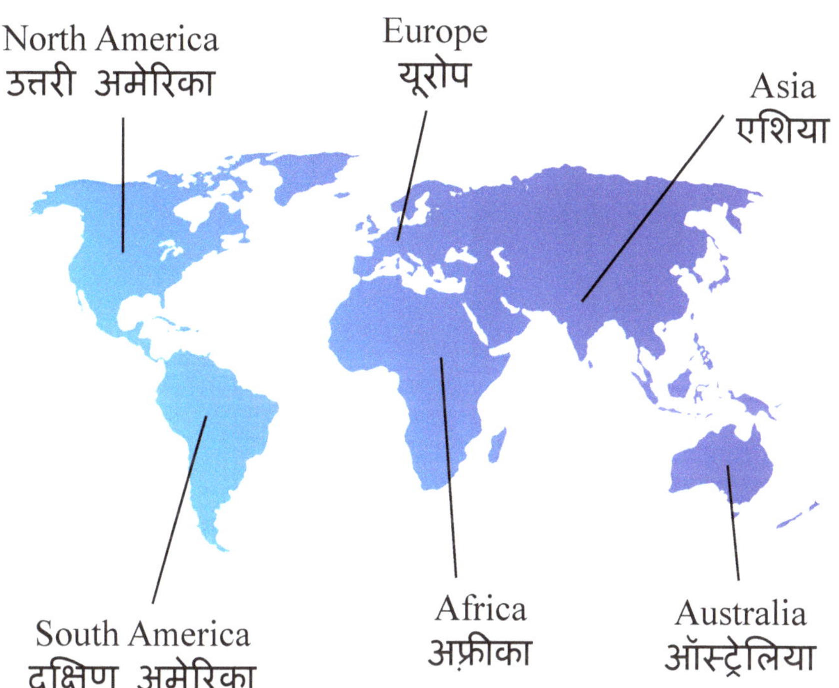

North America
उत्तरी अमेरिका
Europe
यूरोप
Asia
एशिया
South America
दक्षिण अमेरिका
Africa
अफ़्रीका
Australia
ऑस्ट्रेलिया

spring
वसंत

summer
ग्रीष्म

autumn
शरद्

winter
शिशिर

hairdresser
हेयरड्रेसर

florist
फूलवाली

cleaner
सफ़ाई वाला

chef
बावर्ची

waitress
वेट्रेस

musician
संगीत वादक
guitar
गिटार
loudspeaker
स्पीकर

microphone
माइक

reporter
संवाददाता

teacher
अध्यापक